# How to use this workbook

This workbook consists of structured exercises in the joining technique, which teaches a step-by-step approach to joined-up handwriting. It is essential that the writer starts with the baseline joins and progresses through the levels as shown in the workbook. Encourage the writer to follow the direction indicated. This will keep the writer in the correct place for the next joining letter. The writer should trace over each letter with a pencil or pen and practise writing the letters in the spaces provided. Short, but daily practice sessions of 10 minutes are recommended to help improve writing speed.

## Key

●    Indicates the starting point of the letter and also the relocation of the pencil (pencil lift)

→    Indicates the direction the writer should follow

⏃    Indicates the return direction for the writer to follow (bounce)

## How you can help

The Morrells Handwriting write-in practice workbooks are designed for children to work through independently.

However, adult supervision is recommended to ensure the following:

- Good sitting position with both feet flat on the floor, knees at 90°, bottom touching the back of the chair, leaning slightly forward and chair pulled into the desk.
- The correct grip. The dynamic tripod grip with thumb and index finger on pencil. Place the middle finger underneath the pencil with the last two fingers tucked out of the way to help the writer to write for longer without pain.
- A relaxed grip for fluent handwriting and to prevent tired hands.
- The writer must trace over all the letters to ensure correct letter shape and direction.
- The paper is tilted in the correct position with both arms on the table.

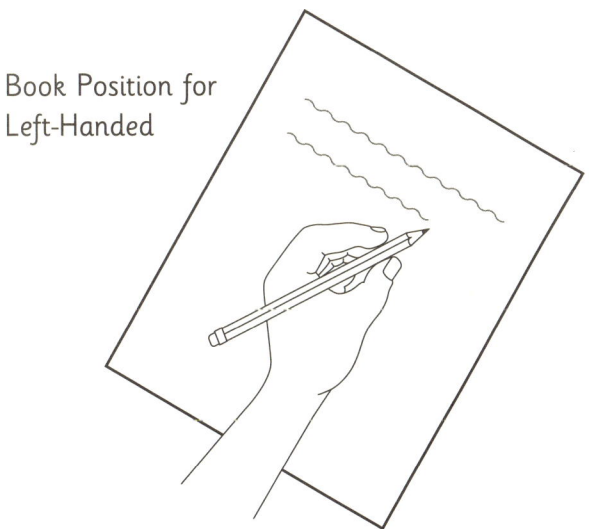

Book Position for Left-Handed

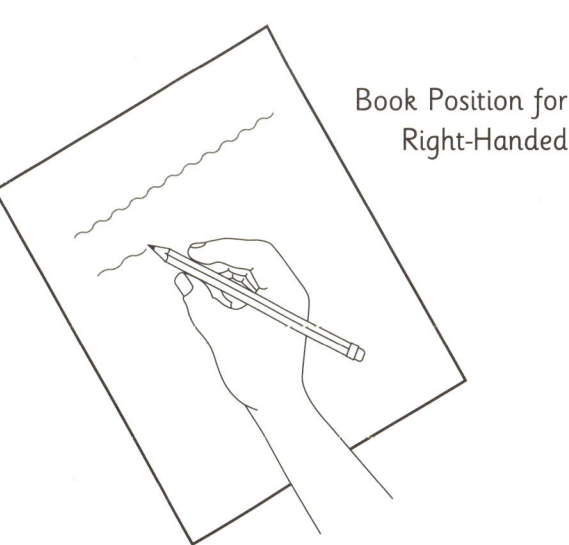

Book Position for Right-Handed

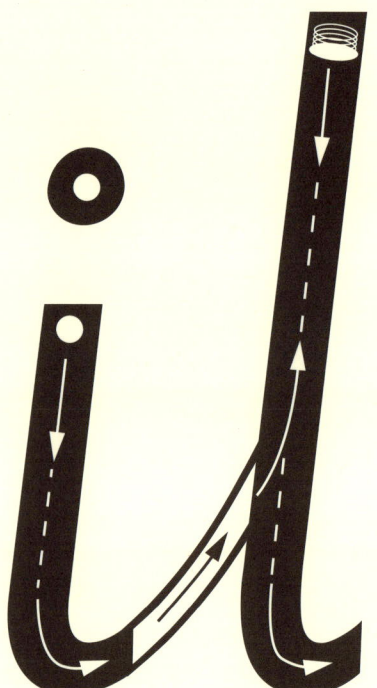

Level 1 : Baseline Joins

Date _____

✏️ **Look at the letters above. Write over the letters below.**

✏️ **Write over the letters below.**   ✏️ **Now practise writing the letters below.**

✏️ **Write over the letters below. Now practise writing the letters below.**

4  Joining Letters workbook 1    © Morrells Handwriting. Photocopying prohibited. All rights reserved.

Level 1 : Baseline Joins

Date _____

✏️ **Look at the letters above. Write over the letters below.**

✏️ **Write over the letters below.**   ✏️ **Now practise writing the letters below.**

✏️ **Write over the letters below. Now practise writing the letters below.**

Joining Letters workbook 1

Level 1 : Baseline Joins

Date _____

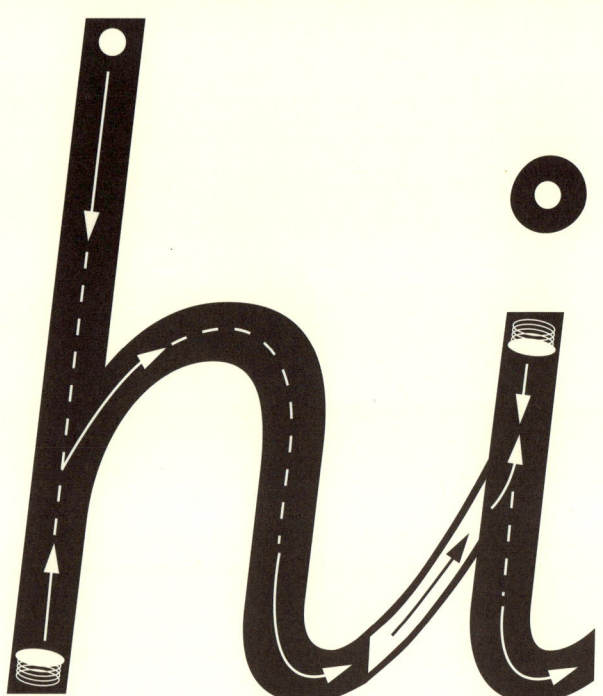

✎ **Look at the letters above. Write over the letters below.**

✎ **Write over the letters below.**     ✎ **Now practise writing the letters below.**

✎ **Write over the letters below. Now practise writing the letters below.**

6     Joining Letters workbook 1     © Morrells Handwriting. Photocopying prohibited. All rights reserved.

Level 1 : Baseline Joins

Date

✏️ Look at the letters above. Write over the letters below.

✏️ Write over the letters below.     ✏️ Now practise writing the letters below.

✏️ Write over the letters below. Now practise writing the letters below.

Joining Letters workbook 1

Level 1 : Baseline Joins

Date

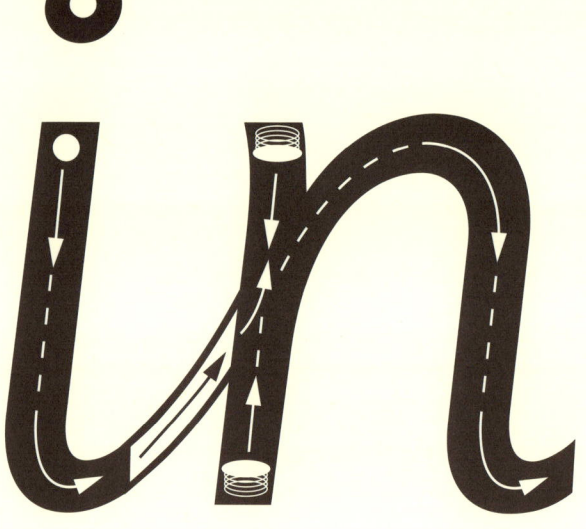

✏️ **Look at the letters above. Write over the letters below.**

✏️ **Write over the letters below.**   ✏️ **Now practise writing the letters below.**

✏️ **Write over the letters below. Now practise writing the letters below.**

8   Joining Letters workbook 1   © Morrells Handwriting. Photocopying prohibited. All rights reserved.

Level 1 : Baseline Joins

Date _____

**Look at the letters above. Write over the letters below.**

*mu    mu    mu    mu    mu*

*mu    mu    mu    mu    mu*

**Write over the letters below.**              **Now practise writing the letters below.**

*mu    mu*                                      *mu    mu*

*mu    mu*                                      *mu    mu*

**Write over the letters below. Now practise writing the letters below.**

*mu    mu*

*mu    mu*

 © Morrells Handwriting. Photocopying prohibited. All rights reserved.    Joining Letters workbook 1    9

Level 1 : Baseline Joins

Date _____

**Look at the letters above. Write over the letters below.**

un    un    un    un    un

un    un    un    un    un

**Write over the letters below.**                **Now practise writing the letters below.**

un    un                                          un    un

uny   uny                          uny   uny

**Write over the letters below. Now practise writing the letters below.**

uny   uny

uny   uny

Level 2 : Round Joins

Date

**Look at the letters above. Write over the letters below.**

cc     cc     cc     cc     cc

cc     cc     cc     cc     cc

**Write over the letters below.**          **Now practise writing the letters below.**

cc     cc     cc                           cc     cc

cco    cco                                 cco    cco

**Write over the letters below. Now practise writing the letters below.**

cco    cco

cco    cco

Joining Letters workbook 1

Level 2 : Round Joins

Date _____

**Look at the letters above. Write over the letters below.**

*ca    ca    ca    ca    ca*

*ca    ca    ca    ca    ca*

**Write over the letters below.**     **Now practise writing the letters below.**

*ca    ca              ca    ca*

*cao   cao             cao   cao*

**Write over the letters below. Now practise writing the letters below.**

*cao   cao*

*cao   cao*

Level 2 : Round Joins

Date

**Look at the letters above. Write over the letters below.**

ds   ds   ds   ds   ds

ds   ds   ds   ds   ds

**Write over the letters below.**            **Now practise writing the letters below.**

ds                                            ds   ds

dsq   dsq                                     dsq   dsq

**Write over the letters below. Now practise writing the letters below.**

dsq   dsq

dsq   dsq

Joining Letters workbook 1

Level 2 : Round Joins

Date

**Look at the letters above. Write over the letters below.**

*ad   ad   ad   ad   ad*

*ad   ad   ad   ad   ad*

**Write over the letters below.**    **Now practise writing the letters below.**

*ad   ad                    ad   ad*

*ade   ade           ade   ade*

**Write over the letters below. Now practise writing the letters below.**

*ade   ade*

*ade   ade*

Level 2 : Round Joins

Date

**Look at the letters above. Write over the letters below.**

**Write over the letters below.**   **Now practise writing the letters below.**

**Write over the letters below. Now practise writing the letters below.**

Joining Letters workbook 1   15

Level 2 : Round Joins

Date

**Look at the letters above. Write over the letters below.**

ee  ee  ee  ee  ee

ee  ee  ee  ee  ee

**Write over the letters below.**   **Now practise writing the letters below.**

ee  ee  ee  ee

eed  eed  eed  eed

**Write over the letters below. Now practise writing the letters below.**

eed  eed

eed  eed

Level 2 : Round Joins

Date

**Look at the letters above. Write over the letters below.**

as    as    as    as    as

as    as    as    as    as

**Write over the letters below.**  **Now practise writing the letters below.**

as    as        as    as

asp    asp        asp    asp

**Write over the letters below. Now practise writing the letters below.**

asp    asp

asp    asp

Joining Letters workbook 1

Level 2 : Round Joins

Date

**Look at the letters above. Write over the letters below.**

de  de  de  de

de  de  de  de

**Write over the letters below.**  **Now practise writing the letters below.**

de  de  de  de

deb  deb  deb  deb

**Write over the letters below. Now practise writing the letters below.**

deb  deb

deb  deb

Level 2 : Round Joins

Date

**Look at the letters above. Write over the letters below.**

sc   sc   sc   sc   sc

sc   sc   sc   sc   sc

**Write over the letters below.**   **Now practise writing the letters below.**

sc   sc      sc   sc

sch   sch      sch   sch

**Write over the letters below. Now practise writing the letters below.**

sch   sch

sch   sch

Joining Letters workbook 1

Level 2 : Round Joins

Date

**Look at the letters above. Write over the letters below.**

da   da   da   da   da

da   da   da   da   da

**Write over the letters below.**         **Now practise writing the letters below.**

da   da                da   da

dag dag                dag dag

**Write over the letters below. Now practise writing the letters below.**

dag dag

dag dag

Level 3 : Top Joins

Date

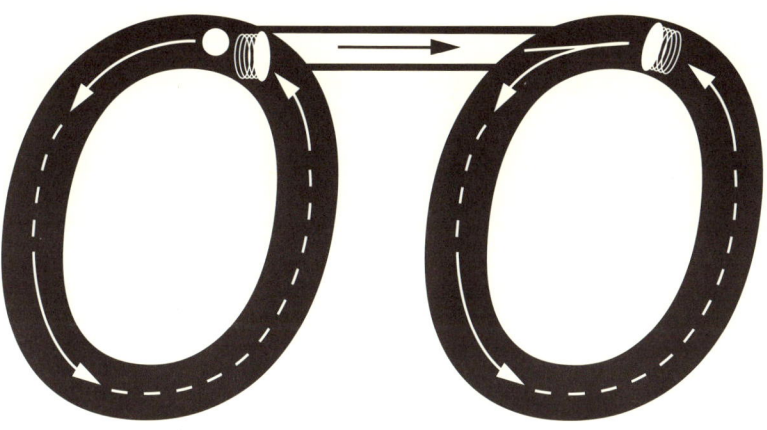

**Look at the letters above. Write over the letters below.**

**Write over the letters below.**     **Now practise writing the letters below.**

**Write over the letters below. Now practise writing the letters below.**

Level 3 : Top Joins

Date _____

**Look at the letters above. Write over the letters below.**

on    on    on    on

on    on    on    on

**Write over the letters below.**   **Now practise writing the letters below.**

on    on           on    on

one   one          one   one

**Write over the letters below. Now practise writing the letters below.**

one   one

one   one

22   Joining Letters workbook 1      © Morrells handwriting. Photocopying prohibited. All rights reserved.

Level 3 : Top Joins

Date _____

**Look at the letters above. Write over the letters below.**

**Write over the letters below.**   **Now practise writing the letters below.**

**Write over the letters below. Now practise writing the letters below.**

Joining Letters workbook 1

Level 3 : Top Joins

Date

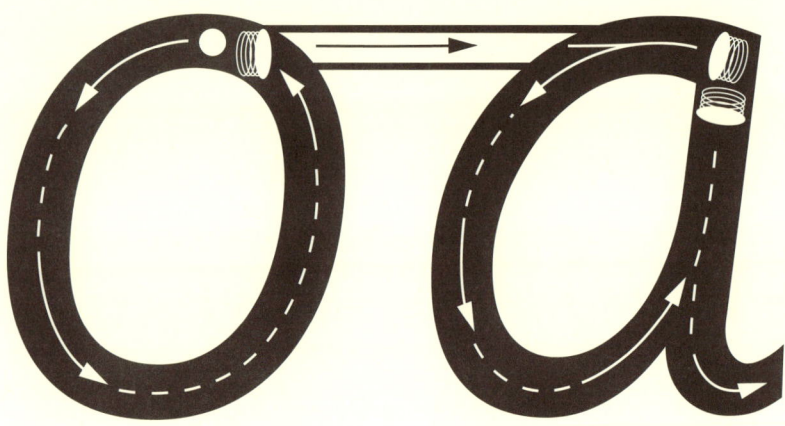

Look at the letters above. Write over the letters below.

Write over the letters below.   Now practise writing the letters below.

Write over the letters below. Now practise writing the letters below.

24  Joining Letters workbook 1   © Morrells Handwriting. Photocopying prohibited. All rights reserved.

Level 3 : Top Joins

Date

**Look at the letters above. Write over the letters below.**

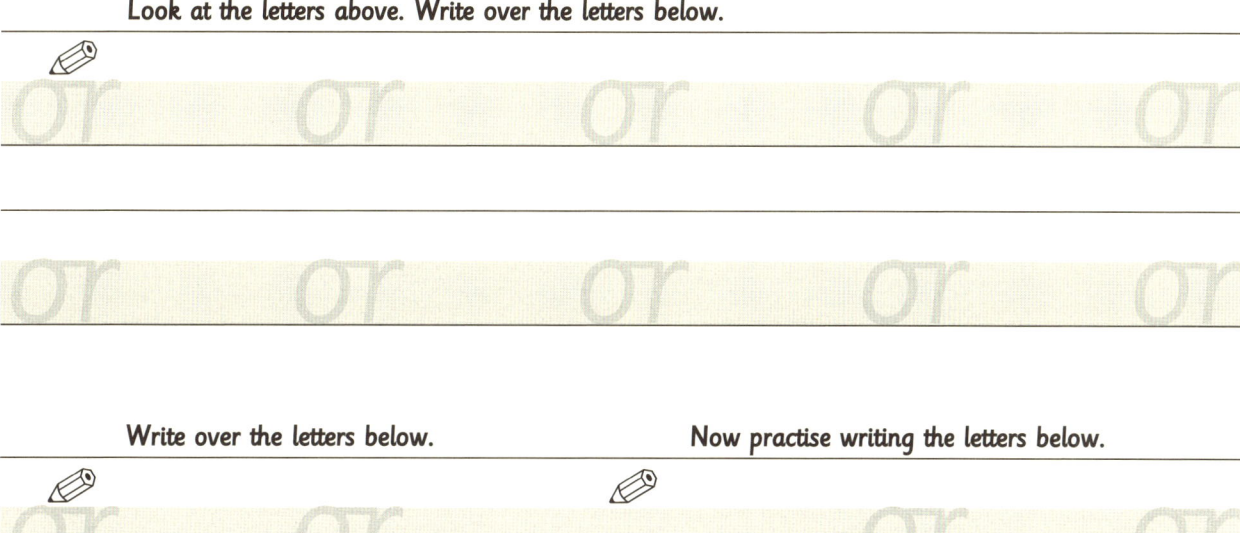

Write over the letters below.  Now practise writing the letters below.

Write over the letters below. Now practise writing the letters below.

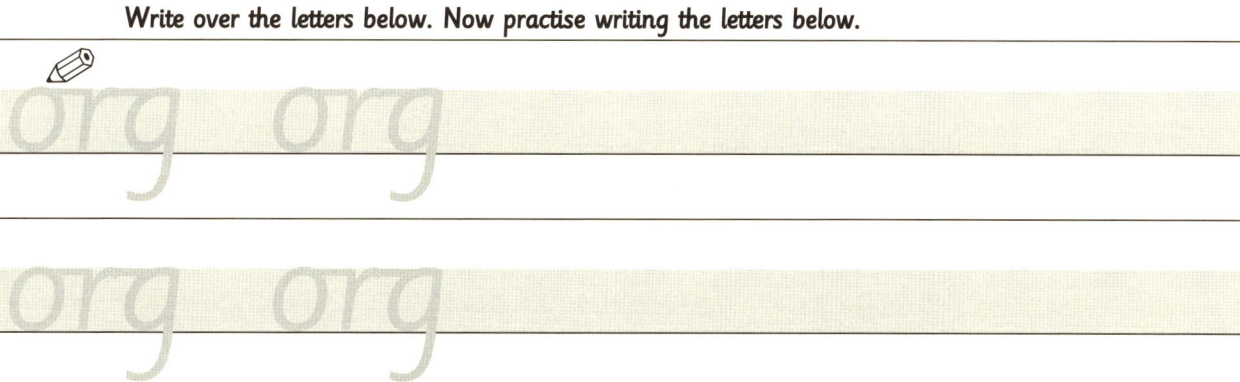

Joining Letters workbook 1   25

# Level 3 : Top Joins

Date _____

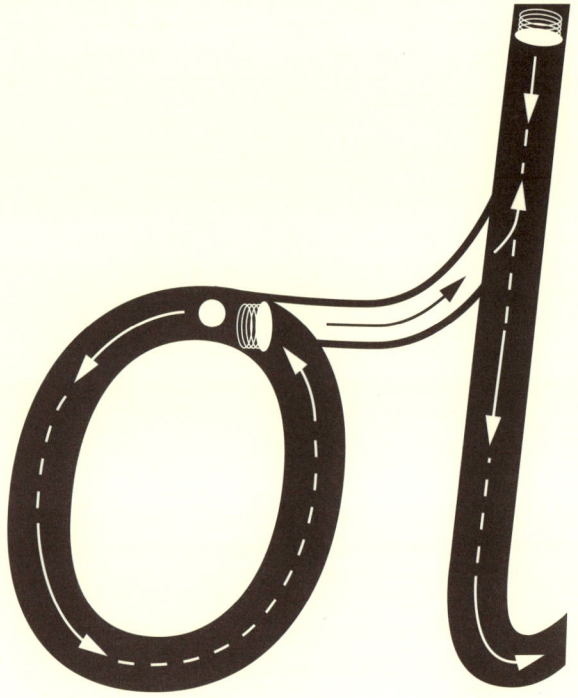

**Look at the letters above. Write over the letters below.**

ol    ol    ol    ol    ol

ol    ol    ol    ol    ol

**Write over the letters below.**   **Now practise writing the letters below.**

ol    ol    ol    ol    ol

old    old    old    old

**Write over the letters below. Now practise writing the letters below.**

old    old

old    old

26   Joining Letters workbook 1    © Morrells Handwriting. Photocopying prohibited. All rights reserved.

Level 3 : Top Joins

Date

**Look at the letters above. Write over the letters below.**

ri  ri  ri  ri  ri

ri  ri  ri  ri  ri

**Write over the letters below.**  **Now practise writing the letters below.**

ri  ri  ri  ri

rid  rid  rid  rid

**Write over the letters below. Now practise writing the letters below.**

rid  rid

rid  rid

© Morrells Handwriting. Photocopying prohibited. All rights reserved.   Joining Letters workbook 1

Level 3 : Top Joins

Date _____

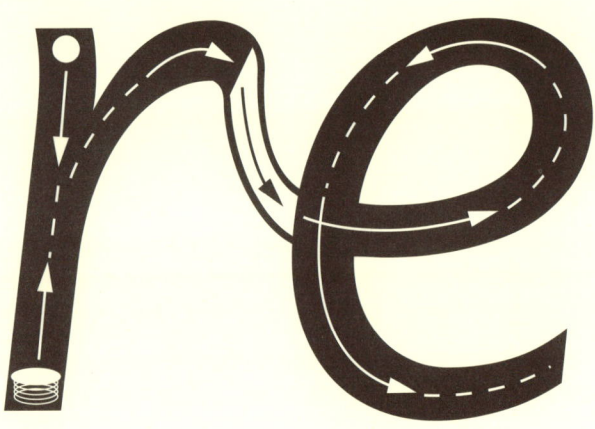

**Look at the letters above. Write over the letters below.**

re    re    re    re    re

re    re    re    re    re

**Write over the letters below.**     **Now practise writing the letters below.**

re    re                re    re

res   res               res   res

**Write over the letters below. Now practise writing the letters below.**

res   res

res   res

28    Joining Letters workbook 1    © Morrells Handwriting. Photocopying prohibited. All rights reserved.

Level 3 : Top Joins

Date

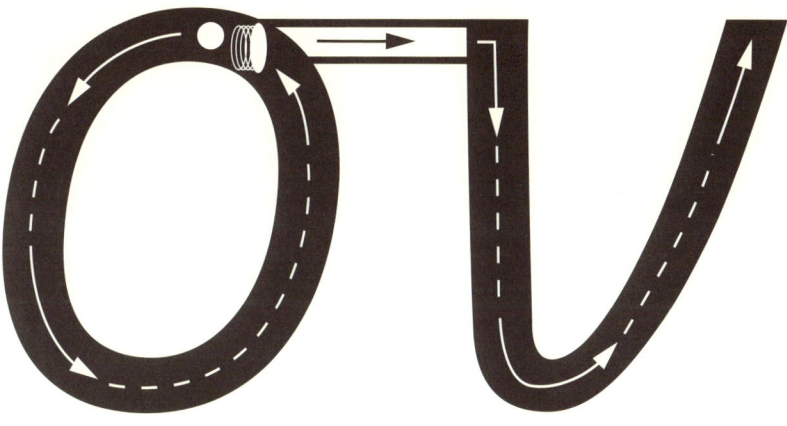

**Look at the letters above. Write over the letters below.**

**Write over the letters below.**   **Now practise writing the letters below.**

**Write over the letters below. Now practise writing the letters below.**

Joining Letters workbook 1   29

Level 3 : Top Joins

Date

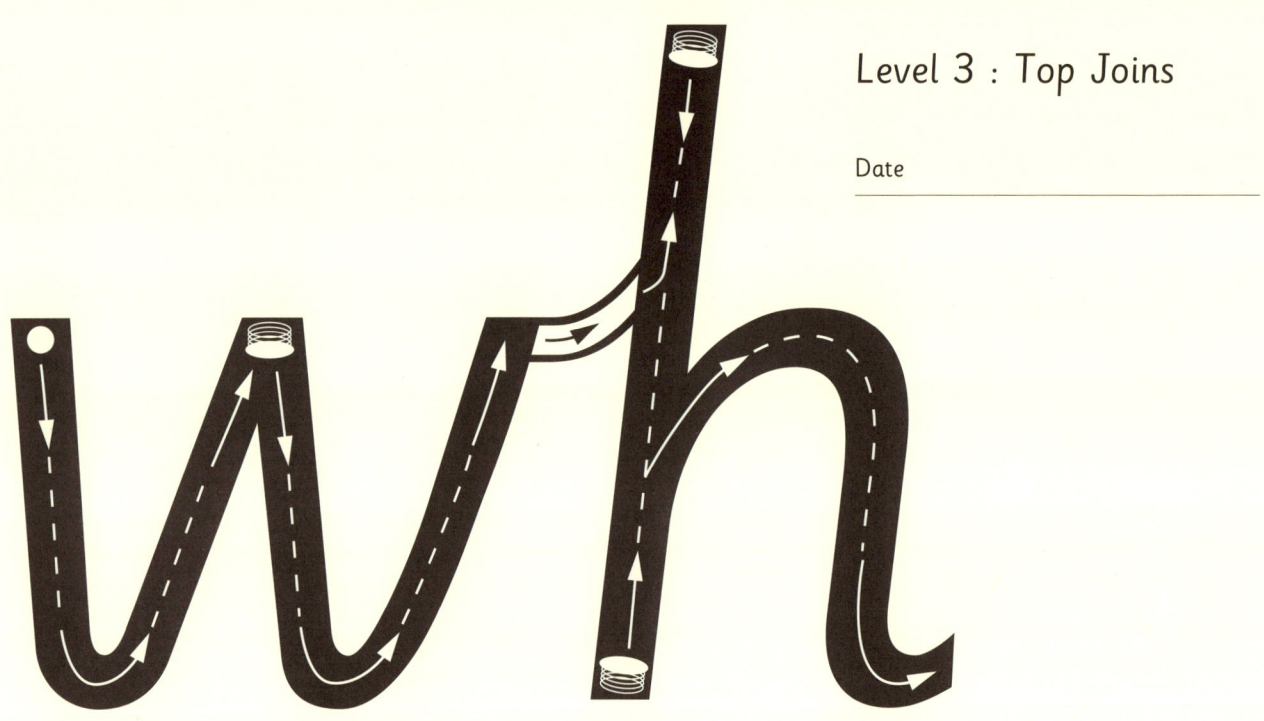

**Look at the letters above. Write over the letters below.**

wh   wh   wh   wh   wh

wh   wh   wh   wh   wh

**Write over the letters below.**     **Now practise writing the letters below.**

wh   wh                    wh   wh

whs   whs                  whs   whs

**Write over the letters below. Now practise writing the letters below.**

whs   whs

whs   whs

Level 3 : Top Joins

Date

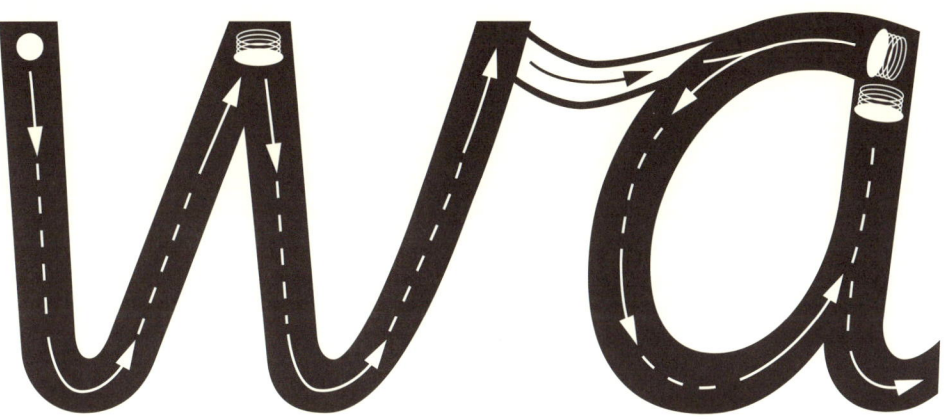

**Look at the letters above. Write over the letters below.**

wa   wa   wa   wa   wa

wa   wa   wa   wa   wa

**Write over the letters below.**  **Now practise writing the letters below.**

wa   wa                          wa   wa

was was                          was was

**Write over the letters below. Now practise writing the letters below.**

was was

was was

Joining Letters workbook 1

Level 3 : Top Joins

Date

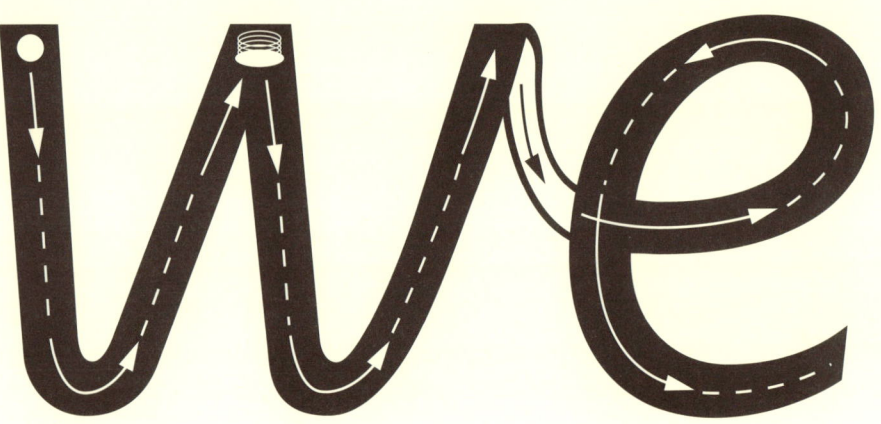

**Look at the letters above. Write over the letters below.**

we  we  we  we  we

we  we  we  we  we

**Write over the letters below.    Now practise writing the letters below.**

we  we         we  we

wer  wer       wer  wer

**Write over the letters below. Now practise writing the letters below.**

wer  wer

wer  wer

Level 3 : Top Joins

Date _____

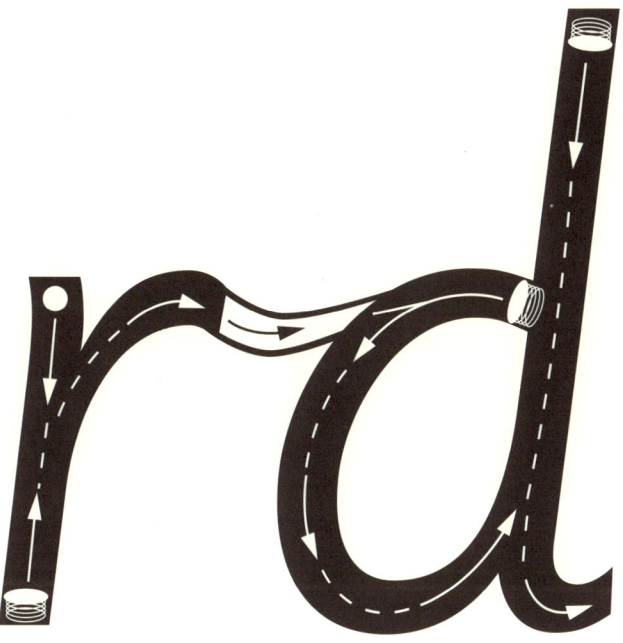

**Look at the letters above. Write over the letters below.**

rd   rd   rd   rd   rd

rd   rd   rd   rd   rd

**Write over the letters below.**          **Now practise writing the letters below.**

rd   rd   rd

rds   rds   rds   rds

**Write over the letters below. Now practise writing the letters below.**

rds   rds

rds   rds

Joining Letters workbook 1

Level 3 : Top Joins

Date _____

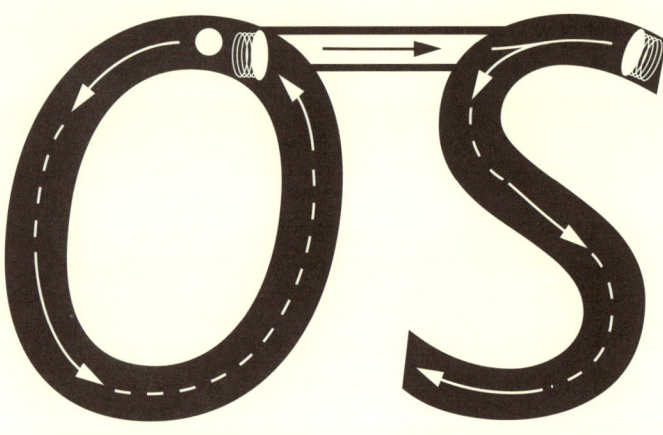

Look at the letters above. Write over the letters below.

Write over the letters below.     Now practise writing the letters below.

Write over the letters below. Now practise writing the letters below.